Colours of Poetry

NUMBER ONE

by

Colin Michael

Cover Painting by Colin Michael

ISBN: ISBN: 9798582282181
Imprint: Independently published
Colours of Poetry by Colin Michael 2020

Contents

Thirty-five Poems taken from many years of writing. They are ranging from short humorous thoughts and observations to present day multimedia that influence and shape the world we live in today. Thought provoking.

Colin Michael 17th December 2017

1

Bubble gum wrapper

A bubble gum wrapper lay crumpled upon the ground
Until a brisk breeze picked it up to throw it around

Moving this way and that it continued to flit and float
Until a depression helped it to fall down into a moat

The bubble gum wrapper lay sodden upon the bank
Until a small animal came with thirst it drank

It sucked in the sweet wrapper with great delight
Not realising that its demise was now in sight.

2

Door mouse

I lay half-awake my eyes still closed
Listening to sounds as the sun hit my toes
The warmth spilled over and into the house
Creaking floorboards sprang back into life

I could hear the sounds of the waking cars
Coughing spluttering metal monsters from Mars
Then the clunk of the hot water pipes sounds
Gurgling and pumping its heat all around

I have to get up out of my warm bed
I couldn't be bothered a voice spoke instead
It was the door mouse larger than life
I could not believe it I turned to my wife

Still fast asleep content with her dreams
I twisted and turned with great difficulty it seems
Coming to terms with a talking mouse in my head
Conveying its displeasure about my squeaking bed.

3

Happy days

Vanilla ice cream tubs
Wooden spoons
Sandy beaches
Orange flip flops
Sunny blue skies
Rubber dolphin rings
Castle shaped buckets
Warm breaking seas
Colourful windbreakers
Sand dunes of grass
Jellyfish not to stroke
Waves to dive through
Mum's homemade lemonade
Dad down the pub
Fish & chips mushy peas
Sister buried in a book
I dig pointless sandy holes
Rock pools full of life
Sunsets over the sea
Time to head home for tea
Mother tugs at my wet costume
Revealing my dignity for all to see
Climb into the car smelling of sea
The long drive home to nice cup of tea
Slipped into a lovely comforting warm bed
To dream of fighting pirates and ships
Treasure Island's boxes of gold doubloons
Happy summer days gone by.

4

Clouds over Europe

Blacken clouds thicken covering Europe again
I can't believe history is about to repeat itself
What is the point of educating the youth
When all they do is follow the app of self-destruct

There must be an emoji that says follow me over the cliff
Our fathers must be turning in burnt ashes of despair
Who did what who did when just look at me now
It's more important to appear on YouTube or in a reality
show

A game to be played out on your mobile phone
It's about being on MTV now not tomorrow
We are all totally media lead by assassination of facts
Falling on deafened ears blasted into the stratosphere

With concentration at an unprecedented all time low
The need to own the latest gadget to impress your
personal ego
I fear for us all but who cares what I think write or
capture
It can't be important after all it's only life.

5

Connectability

Text me
WhatsApp me
Email me
Messenger me
Google me
Facebook me
YouTube me
Video call me
Twitter me
But for god sake don't phone me
I might be doing something
You don't want to know about
On the other hand
Drop me a note
Old fashioned letter
Pigeon carrier
Send a man servant
Here is my card
I request your presence
Tea and cucumber crust free triangles
After all
I just want to meet you
Get to know you
Hold your gaze
Your hand
Or is that too bold
Is this too forward
Too quick
If you can't do the above
I'm not too sure what to do.

Give me a sign
A gesture
One that I can compute
And not misread
I would hate to offend
Intentions are honourable
But are they
The darkened web
A place a face to hide.

6

Reflections

I reflect on a forgotten way
When I could sit out and lay
To feel the warm sun
Beating down upon my brow

Alas but not today
It's another English grey day
Northern lights don't burn so bright
I long for Africa's full warm light

Run as a child through open space
Not cluttered by humanity's waste
Longing for those lost golden ways
When simplicity was order of day

Reflecting on childhood past
Flickering though a Cinematic delight
I wander through my thoughts
Remembering joyest time no stress

Jumping out of jacaranda trees
Only to fall to my knees
Nothing new my mother says
Germolene to smooth away the graze

Now to watch the storm gather its pace
Purple black clouds appear to race
Sweet smells of rain thunder clap light blaze
Birds and animals take shelter in haste.

I too am summoned inside
Face pressed hard on pane of glass
To watch the rain cascade and splash
Like pearls of glass hitting the grass

As soon as it came it moves on again
Time to enjoy puddles that remain
To splash through the sodden street
With suns blistering bright with heat

Thoughts of the heady distant past
Not seen through rose tinted glass
A small tear wells up in the corner of my eye
To tumble fall like joy of sunny days

I can still remember before I disembark
The smell of Africa like no other I remark
To those who were not born on this soil
The meaning of what can move your soul

If I can have a final wish in this life
It's to be scattered upon the cradle of life
To be returned to the place I hold dear
Would make me so happy without fear.

7

Self-destruction

I drank and drank
With all my might

To erase the past
With one pint

It only achieved the
Worst problems of all

There's no difference between
Ceiling or floor.

8

I am a bat

I am a bat
And I live in Rogers's hat
I don't think he knows
Even when he blows his nose
I hang around in barns
Preferring local organic farms
I once tried a cave
But found it too deprived
I tried my five
Fruit and veg a day
But found it bloated me out
Just like uncle Ted's head
With uncontrollable splurge
I pooped on Roger's head
I said it was not me
Believe me I went on TV
Inappropriate behaviour
Was the media purge
But nobody would believe
They said I did it before
The next thing I knew
I was turned out and flew
My barn days were over
I swooped over fields of clover
Descended to live alone
Eating cider apples and grapes
Getting drunk in appropriate caves
Missing Roger with his funny ways.

9

Quiet and peace

I hear as though another voice
Golden leaves fall tumble to earth

Birds float serenely high above
They are not beauties of hovering love

But devils from far away
Swooping hither to flow and crow

Alas the sun is fading too fast
As do leaves of youthfulness past

Shades of greens fade and wither
Leaving brown shadows do dither

I reflect on distant times past
Remembering only life's difficult task

Darkness arrives so thick and fast
No time to conjure up and reflect on the past

Laying down quietly in one's peace
Pillowed on shortened dewed grass.

10

Look to the heavens

I waited and watched with a furrowed brow
As hunger grew across this town

I looked and searched without relief
As hunger grew with throbbing grief

I dug so deep into the ground
Stomach groaning with guttural sound

I looked to the world in utter distress
As politics played out its ugly press

I watched as oil guns were handed about
As communities fought then got rooted out

I looked to the heavens for clouds of rain
Nothing forthcoming only starvation pain.

11

Where has it all gone

I am finding it hard to control my anger
What with Brexit Catalonia Brussels and all
Or whatever his name is
Political people are messing with my life

I knew where I was going or so I thought
I have no control which I once did have
It's not long ago I had plans
Now I don't any more

The wind of change is afoot
Whatever that means
I had money a house now I don't
It's all been taken away from me

This was never my fault
I sit and gaze out of my sorry flat
At what I don't know
The abyss the depth totally unknown

What a sorry state we are all in
I was told it's to do with the alignment of planets
That's messing with our inner waterworks
Pulling us from poll to poll pillar to post

Where is the logic the history the science in that
Out through the window and in through the door
In my one bed flat spilling to the floor
That's where it has gone wrong.

12

The queue

I queued and queued
For an hour or more,
Only to find they had closed the store

What a waste
That hour that space
To queue forever now losing my place

To leave with zero
Feeling like a deflated hero
I sure did not feel like Robert De Niro.

13

Pebbles by the sea

Looking out as far as you can see
Pebbles skim over breaking waves
Careful to miss the overexcited dog
Dragging a stick and a ball in the mouth
A pop of a champagne bottle as lovers embrace

Brighton rock snaps sweetly into bits
Chips with vinegar in yesterday's news
Knotted hanky order of the day
Deckchairs placed according to the sun
Handbags full of cheese sandwiches and sticky buns

Sea gulls calling out as they dive to steal
Ninety-nine and two chocolate flakes
Small boats bob quietly far out to sea
Fishermen with oily jackets afloat
Anticipating their biggest catch of week

Excitement adrenaline all rolled into one
The blot on the seascape is the old pier
Rusty burnt falling gracefully into the sea
Time to run in and out of breaking waves
While up above children play and laugh

Slot machines oranges and lemons
Coins that never drop down to win
Glassblowers make seahorses in green
Fluffy pink candyfloss spins on a stick
Gobstoppers too big for your mouth

Cup of tea grandma best drink of the day
Grandfather a quick pint of beer
Lay back relax what a wonderful time
Endless waves meet rolling blue skies of joy
Making up a day of frolicking by the sea.

14

Slow cooked

Don't you just like a plate of food
Cooked with all the love in the world
Grandma's recipe from golden days

Spices fresh meat and veg
Collected from the garden and hedges around
Slow cooked or seared to perfection

Good family and company are a must
To colour your palate
Turning it into a culinary feast to delight

All washed down with a glass or two
Of your finest wine is a must
Otherwise it's just another plate of food.

15

Nectar

To bee or not to be
That's the buzz on the street
Roof top gardens with fruit trees
Urban societies are doing their bit

Hanging baskets from your local store
Full of flowers smells colours galore
One after the other they take their turn
To gather the nectar for all concerned

Long flight home coordinates well known
Pouches laden full and heavy
Welcoming committee with open wings
A good day's work for all it seems

The sun sets warmly over the hive
With activity reduced to a murmur inside
The queen lays back content with her day
Moonlight sheds a soft good night.

16

Blind date

I was under duress or was it stress
Not too sure as I put on a new dress

Reflecting on what image to portray
I realised I was running late for my date

Should I wear my hair up or down
You have no idea what dilemmas go around

The phone rings the cab is waiting outside
More pressure as I choose which shoes to wear

Coat handbag make-up a bag full of things
Just a quick double G&T before closing the door

Blind date profile looks good on the website
Hoping he's full of fun to fill an exciting night.

17

Offshore

It's been a wonderful varied checkered career
Looking back it was mostly black and white
Preferred chances I should not have taken

Results that I never saw coming from the blue
Thrills and spills were always there to enjoy
Remembering how to play the winning hand

Watching the eyes for the tell-tale signs
Rewards are something else to savour
Short lived forgotten in an instant of time

Onwards and upwards was the motto of the day
Sit back now you've done your very best
Taxman rears his ugly head to take away your vest

The nest egg you squirreled in a paradise account
Is now deemed illegal even though you were right
The smile on your face has been replaced in disgrace

You lose your house the trophy blonde called the wife
The kids are on your back with university debts for life
Welcome to my wonderful park bench I call home

Keeping warm with my dog discarded smelly rough
clothes
Cap well placed wishing hoping a small donation of
change
The need is real to pop down the local to ease the pain

People offer creative advice not wishing to understand my strife
All coming from a good angel somewhere up there
Sometimes it's meant to be come on down buy me a beer.

18

Whoosh bang

A cold November evening
We stood around all dreaming
The memories flooding thick and fast
Thoughts of colours from my past

The bonfire burns and crackles bright
Flames lick up into the night
We wrote our names as sparklers spit with light
Filling the air with our laughter and fights

Then came the whiz and then a bang
To startle frighten the weary sprang
Sounds pierced small children ears
Then came mum to comfort floods of tears

A fizz a whoosh colours so vibrant bright
Bursting into the darkness so very light
I won't forget happy cold November delight
Ghosts of past that burnt into the night.

19

Lunch break

Reg greeted me as I entered the local park
A beautiful sunny day as children ran around having lark

Ducks playfully paddling up and down or sheltering
under trees
While I found a chair just as the park attendant collected
fees

I pulled out my latest book rescued from the Red Cross
shop
Setting down with bap of ham hock pickles and cheese
on top

It was another lunch time away from the hassle of the
office
To think of nothing no calls no emails no texts I promise

Reg reappeared all happy his wanting eyes wishing me
to play
Threw my ball my stick it's such a lovely sunny day

All too soon it was time to pack up and head back to my
desk
I savour these short times spent alone it helps my
distress.

20

Lush

Lying under canvas in the middle of the night
While all rolled up tight warm snug as a bug
Patter pat of rain drops musically playing their tune

While the rustle of the cows plods quietly past
Flaps of the tent folded back in neat bows
Clouds drift apart to reveal full moon so clear

Shadows create monsters of the summer solstice night
Druids gather on Salisbury plain to dance and chant
While the cows move slowly tearing up lush grass
Cracking spit wood camp fire burns orange bright
Illuminating the inner sanctuary of bell tent of ten
Friends swap stories of childhood camping exploits

While one disturbs the quietness of the night
Up for skinny dipping in the lake beyond
Pin drops no one responds thoughts of cold outside

Or catching glimpses of unmentionable bits
One turns over and other fakes a muttered snort
While the cows reply with a mutated moo no way

Night rolls on into an illuminating warming sunrise
Smells of the fresh dew fluorescent green grass
Steam rises up to fill the crisp blue morning sky
Time to get up to prod poke the fire back to life
Billycan hangover full of spring's purest water
Mug of tea while contemplating my inner peace.

21

Good Morning

Struggled with great difficulty to rise from my bed
Cradling my throbbing extremely heavy head

The taste in my mouth was garlic and wine
Difficulty to remember with whom I did dine

I eventually made it to the bathroom in time
Blessing the porcelain with red ruby divine

Stagger tottering crawling back to my bed
Deciding it's better for my poor heavy head.

22

It was Fate

Mother woke me up as she had ironed my pants
Dad had had his smoked kipper's tea and toast
Tents on the local green was order of the day
Summer fête full colour mostly red blue and white

Mother polyester dressing gown waiting impatiently by
the door
Doreen the mobile hairdresser with tools of torture was
late
Pink Morris minor spluttered crunching up the gravel
drive
With on the backseat a contraption of electrocution
lobotomy or worse

My sister was up nose in a book spooning warm milk
cornflakes
Paying no attention to the bowl as she shovelled spoon
after spoon
Only to look up indignantly at my arrival you stupid boy
Short cropped wavy brown hair red ribbon tied neatly to
one side

Pull your socks up your scruffy little urchin my mother
would say
I tucked into my strawberry coated white toast and milky
tea
The day would be a wonderful excitement of frolic and
fun
Summer sun with smells of fruits animals puppies
perfume and hay.

As per normal the family would leave the house all
holding hands
We must not be late for the local fair that was not done
Opening with pomp by some non-celebrity from London
town
Performed with theatrical overkill preceded by the
ribbon cutting

The aim of the day was to win the tombola big prize a
bottle of lemonade
With half a crown and confidence abound I dipped my
hand into the box
Number twenty-four a winning number I was assured by
Mrs Lovechild
Alas with usual disappoint a Cox apple an orange or a
green fairy cake

Father retires to the beer tent to have his half-light and
bitter
Men in cloth caps talking about tractors and combined
harvesters
Then turn to discuss the new barmaid and her overloud
chest
A source of great excitement and pointing of fingers at
simple Eric

With calamity and distress the summer storm clouds did
appear
Heavens opening symphony clap of thunder bolt of
white light
First World War bell tent shelter from hailstones the size
of grenades.

Women held with pain of death flowery cups saucers
and victory sponge

Pauline Jean remained seated oblivious in the corner of
the cake tent
Porcelain plate full of crumbs hardback opened to a
cornered page ten
No flinch of acknowledgment of mayhem of life
unfolding before her eyes
Engrossed with the tale of Heathcliff or was it Pride and
Prejudice

It was at the end of a perfect day as we trudged muddily
home for tea
Fish fingers frozen chips radio Beatles please please me
oh not again
What more could anyone ask for other than a big dollop
of pink angel delight
Or a wedge of mother's Victoria butter iced sponge first
prize yet again.

23

Traces

I had not switched on my mobile
Thinking I was being so clever
Hiding from multiple platforms out of sight
Under the radar of satellite detection
But to my shock horror and dismay

It's always sending out a message
Whether you like it or not
Big brother is everywhere yet not
Good or bad it does not mind
Every time you cross the digital line

Beware of all text you write
It will appear on someone else's site
Predictive text is the worst of all
Fouling up an innocent message
To appear discriminatory no defence

They are not following your every letter
But software is searching words of dissent
Flagging up this person or that
Be very afraid as I am your big brother
And I am here to stay.

24

More or less

The love you gave
Is equal to the love that you have given
The sum of the whole
Can be calculated in two equal parts
Where there is a will
There is no way
More or less
It is less
My glass is half full
No it's not it's half empty
A positive is always balanced out
By a negative
Therefore equalisation
Is neither here nor there
A reaction
Causes a counter reaction
There's a point to be made
Which in itself is pointless
Does the sun come up every day
Not in the North Pole
Why do you get two full moons
In one month sometimes
Gravity weighs me down
Heat is relative
Because cold can burn
If I drop a stone in the sea
The ripple goes round the earth
How many times
What does it depend on
The size the weight the height

Either or neither
In other words
There are no words to be said
I rest my case
The prosecution may begin
But if the jury is out
Then it can't comeback in
It's out you said
Or did I misunderstand you
Interpretation
Can be Seen from both side
It Depends
Which side of the fence you are on
Or are you on the fence
My head hurts
I want to go to sleep
To rest to sleep to dream.

25

Twist and tumble

The serenity of snow that gently falls from above
Quietly covering all that is around on the ground
Pure individual white flakes link hand in hand
Twist and tumble blown by a whispering breeze
They land as one knitted blanket of woven delight
The gods from above wake up from sleepy slumber
To flick the snow button off from the heavenly wall
Commanding all individual flakes to cease as one
Leaving a wonderland of magical white so bright.

26

Oh no never no more

I came into my local for some peace and quiet
To write and contemplate corners of my life
Alas not tonight it was to be an Irish sing along

Two men sat on stools microphones and coloured lights
The old country the old-fashioned bygone ways
Aged women with orange hair clapped and whooped

Letting it all hang out with abandon no fear
Groupies sang loud killing every note with a pint of beer
With a neatly drawn clover leaf as if a happy tear

Men drank Irish whisky with flavours musty peat
Only to shout out for another round two would appear
Arms aloft waving in unison to the penny whistle

Piercing my senses into submission to join in with the
crowd
Songs with heartfelt words that everyone knew rang out
Injustice potato plight forced eviction and more

I wish I was home in Berry Cork Killarney or anywhere
else
Sailing away to a better life in Boston Sydney and many
more
"Oh no never no more" the happy crowd sang out not so
clear.

27

Hot and bothered

Opening the book that gathered dust on the shelf
At random I picked page forty-two
The picture looked very inviting warm and fulfilling
That's the one for me definitely
I poured over the lines slowly taking in all the delights

Having only thirty minutes to prepare myself
Opening the cupboard full of the spice of life
Realising I was now out of my depth
I plough on filling in the gaps and doing my best
Funny Ramsey never had these premature problems

Turning up the heat believing this would save the day
Only to find I had overcooked the situation
With ten minutes to go I decided to abandon my venture
Picking up the mobile phone and ordering on line
Number 42 13 22 and 69 that will do.

28

Intrepid delight

Waking up looking out of the bedroom window
With a nice warm cup of breakfast tea and toast

The world comes to life with another working day
People jumping on the bus standing room only

Headphones on watching the latest master chef
Teenagers sharing the last video upload prank

While twittering about their last conquests or fight
The elderly stagger on their way to corner surgery

Early risers with bags of shopping in four-wheel trolley
Cluttering up the bus taking the space of another

Red bus rises up coughs blue fumes out the back
Pulling out in front of drivers playing candy crush

While arguing with their estranged second wife
Screeching another near miss avoided by chance

The dust cart beeps as it reverses in the street
Men jump out shouting with candid verbal abuse

Bin lids flung open to reveal green recycling glass
All thrown into the mix of food paper and tin

Lamps from last night still burn bright out of synch
Magpies swoop down to scavenge yesterday's cake

Alarm clock flickers on news of the day
Global warming cabinet shuffle weather all in the mix

Just another day to savour with intrepid delight
Finishing my tea and toast making my way into the
world beyond.

29

Ducking and diving

I pushed my pram down the street
Knocking people off their feet

Such fun I had causing mayhem
While scooting along with Liam

All tucked up in blankets what a relief
No one was aware of the stolen beef

Ducking in and out of alleyways and pubs
Selling to anyone purchasing my grub

The word gets out time to move on
Pandas and plod arriving with a knock

Good day's work now time to buy my crack
Heavenly evening awaits I partake a little smack.

30

Autumn

Walking alone the other night
A small object caught the corner of my sight
A maple leaf floats from above
Ebbing and turning like a dove

Then another whisked quietly by
Returning to slap me in the eye
Eventually drifting to the ground
Descending gracefully slowly down

Lime green and butter scotch brown
Lay together upon the ground
Creating colours of pure wonder delight
This autumn delivers another magical sight.

31

Brushstroke

I stood pondering my next stroke
Would it be blue purple or coke instead

I lay to rest my throbbing head
Then came a pounding upon my bed

Loaded paintbrush hit my colourful floor
A client I hoped with money at my door

Instead a delivery a new sofa bed
Now disturbing losing my thread

Vanishing thoughts from my head
Leaving me to ponder shall I hit my new bed.

32

Ring Ring

Oh God it annoys me that phone
I sit and listen to its monotone

When it rings again my heart misses a beat
Who could it be at this hour for me

Oh God it annoys me lying in bed
With that telephone ringing in my head

I wish to answer but leave it instead
Let me lay peacefully to rest my head.

33

Old Man

He sat in a corner puffing away on his cigarette
Contemplating life and its hidden dark secrets
Pausing for a second as if to have an answer
But only to exhale blue smoke in a laughter
He dragged himself up and headed for the bar
And ordered a whisky coughing up his catarrh
The music filled the bar and spun around his head
Distorting his thoughts confusing the living dead
Peace and quiet is all he wished for
As he enjoyed his last deep draw.

34

A flower

I picked a flower to give to my lover
It smelt so sweet all rosy and fresh
Reminding me of the day we spent
All cuddled up fast asleep in bed

Morning brought light into our lives
Breakfast hot tea butter and toast
Warm embrace then up and shower
New experiences lay before outside

Leaving together the door slams shut
The tube the bus the walk to work
Texting each other with every move
Arriving at the office no time to waste

I picked a flower to give to my lover
It smelt so sweet all rosy and fresh
Memories of that evening that night
Love intoxicatingly full on with life.

35

Colourful flies

Seasonal changes are such a delight
Especially when the midges come out to bite
Standing in a river legs cold so tight
Ghillie points out still pools clear so bright
Salmon rest before moving on to fight
Best rod with colourful flies to be right
It's going to be a day of fishing delight.

Biography

Colin Michael
Artist, Poet, YouTube Video Maker.

Born in Bulawayo in 1959.
Lived in Salisbury (Harare), Southern Rhodesia
(Zimbabwe) 1959-66.
Emigrated to London, England in 1966.
Emigrated to Paris, France 2018.

Education.
Alfred Beit School, Mabelreign, Southern Rhodesia.
(Zimbabwe)
Middleton Rose Hill, Sutton, London.
Boughton Monchelsea Maidstone Kent.
Biggin Hill, Bromley, Kent.
Churchill School, Westerham, Kent.
Ravensbourne Art College BA Hons.
Slade School of Art, London.

Awards.
D&AD Gold
Evening Standard, Best Advertisements

Paperchase, Best Brochure
The London Group, Best New Artist selected by Albert
Irvin RA

Solo and Group Exhibitions.
1987 to present day-London and Paris.

Associations past and present.
Treasurer, Hon' Member National Society of Painters
Sculptors & Printmakers.
The Arts Club, Mayfair, London
Who's Who in Art.

Currently living and working in Paris.

Kindle epublishing on Amazon
Colours of Poetry, Number One. *17.12.2017*
Colours of Poetry II, Painting with words. *10.03.2020*
Colours of Poetry III, No rhythm nor reason. *20.04.2020*
Tea & Poetry. The First 100 works from 'Colours of
poetry'. *06.05.2020*
Colours of Poetry IV, Pros and cons. *22.05.2020*
Colours of Poetry V, Paradoxically seeking. *20.06.2020*
Colours of Poetry VI, Ambiguous parodies. *20.08.2020*
Colours of Poetry VII. And then some. 30.10.2020
Coffee & Poetry. The Second 100 works from 'Colours
of poetry'. 12.*11.2020*